ella zelensky

Divine Decree **By Ella Zelensky**

Dedication

to sophia,

you were born a warrior and born to change the world. it is an honour to know you and i am excited to see you turn heads as you help make this world a better place with your astonishing knowledge and love. stay curious. stand strong.

ella zelensky

you ask if you
can change the world
if you're asking that
question
then you've already
been making plans
to do so

divine decree

also by ella zelensky

Little Dreamer

© Ella Zelensky, 2021. All Rights Reserved

table of contents

prisoner 13
kind eyes 14
confined 16
turning 18
lunch 20
neglect 22
under the spotlight 23
acknowledgement 24
rejection 25
classroom door 26
out of order 28
emotions 30
shove 31
far away 32
limbo 33
13 years old 34
hallway 35
absence note 36
bus route 37
glass wall 38
choking 39
lifeless 40
jewellery box 41
disco light 42
explosion 44
someone 45
violence 46
ringing teachers 48
to exist 49

table of contents

intrusive 50
kind heart 51
teacup 52
statue 53
class quiz 54
sign language book 56
therapy 57
attentiveness 58
escape 59
rest 60
to be chosen 61
applause 62
never be the reason 63
cater 64
hold the door 65
avoidance 66
seizure 67
water 68
osaka airport 70
mute 72
cut off 73
fear 74
psychosis 75
glitch 76
auditory hallucination 78
paranoia 80
shriek 81
swapped 82
zombies 83

table of contents

jamais vu	84
adulthood	85
stars	86
be considerate	88
not sure	92
radiate	93
end of the day	94
done	95
the end of year 12	96
upset	97
conquering the enemy	98
to stay	99
creatures	100
ignorance	102
catch	104
expectations	105
distress	106
underwater ballet	107
association	108
give, always	109
new day	110
the key	111
affirmation letter	112
the coping	113
leaving school	114
willingness	115
reversed progress	116
life beyond school	117
leave	118

table of contents

mistake 119
undoing 120
"she's the one" 121
broken up 122
confession 123
like versus love 124
periphery 125
making moves 126
'attractive' traits 127
crumble 128
player 129
to leave 130
failed attempt 131
speak up 132
get ready 133
museum 134
ideal 135
western "love" 136
eradication 137
the truth 138
drug 139
differentiate 140
recognising 141
the right person 142
grievance 143
discussion 144
logic 145
mirror image 146
lazy 147

table of contents

support 148
painful wait 149
reckless 150
false affirmation 151
genuine friendship 152
cure 153
mixed features 154
a change of mind 156
irony 157
universal 158
dismantling 159
it exists 160
both sides 161
the mind of a child 162
you don't know how to write 163
convinced 164
assignments 165
abc or humanity? 166
"strange mind" 167
cut-off 168
valid contributions 169
medical condition 170
take that 171
academic award badges 172
the voice of potential 173
hourglass 174
"are you with it?" 175
victory 176
song writing 177

table of contents

silent battle	178
male suicide	179
two friends	180
murder	181
exchange	182
leap	183
too much	184
desperate	185
disappearance	186
ever waiting	187
save	188
an end and a start	189
fearless compassion	190
shaking hands	191
the right friendships	192
microphone	193
it's okay	194
motherhood	195
mother's eyes	196
tatay ko (my father)	197
lola ko (my grandma)	198
tribute	199
ancestors	200
vow	201
spending time	202
recall	203
beloved mama	204
the rows of children	205
drowned	206

table of contents

white noise	207
eyelashes	208
warriors	210
repeating memory	211
orphanage	212
bias	213
the death of the silenced	214
heartless	215
overexposed	216
chance	217
eternally	218
outcast	219
qualification	220
interracial parents	221
protests	222
the realm of souls	223
ascended	224
wait for me	225
reunion	226
we will know	227
confirmation	228
to dare	229
masquerade	230
true selves	231
courtship	232
spinning	233
mysterious impact	234
garden maze	236
aching	237

table of contents

eye contact 238
embrace 239
to requite 240
fear 241
effortless 242
to yearn 243
confession 244
wide eyed 245
changed 246
conflicted desire 247
message 248
trusting 249
to trust 250
opposites 251
i believed 252
the next chapter 254
honesty 256
reaction 257
evolving 258
the ability 259
trust 260
river 261
quiet night 262
patience 263
prayer 264
divine decree 265
finish line 266
afterword 267
about the author 268

ella zelensky

prisoner

they tell me to run
but with each beat of my foot
to the ground
i see my pain flash before my eyes
run, move forward they say
but it's like someone has grabbed me
by the head and is forcing my eyes open
to watch the replay of
my most hurtful moments
and when i grow too tired
and my eyes finally close
the light of the film still shifts
in and out across the side of my face
run they say
but they know very well
that i'll trip and fall halfway

kind eyes

your memory
springs up in
every place
illuminated by
the sun
it is a gentle
memory
and i get caught
between smiling
and crying
no one can see you
while they're walking
but i can
and you're smiling back at me

ella zelensky

divine decree

confined

she was touched by rain
but never by love
warmed by morning
but never by embrace
looked in the eyes
but never seen
and this hurt her
this silenced her
for how could one enter
the outside world when
their room loved them the most

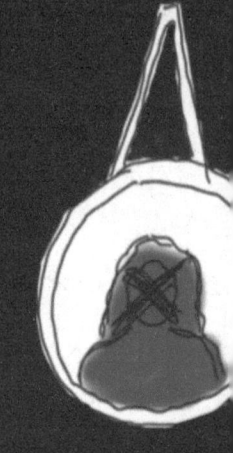

turning

turning around
is so profound
when your eyes
speak for you
and the rest
is no sound

By Ella Zelensky

lunch

a girl sat at the lowest
part of the school
eating lunch alone with
her hat tucked over her face
i was standing still
my eyes examining her
slow and tired
movements
she couldn't sit by herself
and neither could i
so i went down to sit with her
and we saved each other

ella zelensky

neglect

people yelled at him
raising from their seats
throwing accusations
and his anger and sadness
rose and rose and rose
until he fired back, upset
i'm not doing anything wrong!
stop making fun of me!
but nobody cared
the boy who asked for hugs
but was avoided
who knew the essence
of life
but wasn't listened to
he was rejected by everyone
he screamed back
to hell with you all!
and ran away
and i held back tears
as the class was happy he left
and looking around the room
for the approval of their opinion

under the spotlight

deep down
it was their child self
the one who didn't have the
vocabulary to explain
what their condition was
but knew very
very well how it
made them feel

acknowledgement

    i am your witness

rejection

she spun around and said
*i don't want you
to sit with us anymore*
and walked away quickly
groups sitting in the courtyard
looked horrified and sympathetic
standing from their seats and
coming over to me, saying
oh my god, are you okay?
i pursed my lips, tears forming
yeah was all i could say
but i ran upstairs hiccupping
my sadness away
i dashed into the library
and headed for the nearest
corner
so i could sit down
cry
and figure out what to do
for the rest of the year

classroom door

i was the last to leave the classroom
but those three girls
wouldn't let me open the door
they held the doorknob
so i couldn't twist it open
and leave
can't open the door?
they laughed
shaking the doorknob
staring me straight in the eyes
go on they said
open it
open it
open the door
then they let go of it quickly
and ran away, laughing
i walked back to my homeroom
my head hung low
until my legs carried me
back to the girls' bathrooms

ella zelensky

out of order

those first few days
i couldn't believe
what was happening to me
it was new
and it was lonely
my senses picked up everything
and my back pressed against
the cold brick wall
is that toilet stall out of order?
people eventually asked
must be friends would reply
i would hear groups of friends
enter and exit the bathrooms
laughing, chatting
i would hear about their
after school catch ups
group gossip
funny moments at lunch
it was normal for them
and i cried, imagining
what it would be like
to sit with just someone
but i was living in a little toilet stall
that was out of order
for 3 years

ella zelensky

emotions

i can't keep up
with the fluctuations

shove

two girls whispered to each other
glaring at me in a way that told me
that they were going to
do something to me in the hallway
one of them drifted over
as we were walking opposite directions
and shoved me onto the wall
my satchel slipped off my shoulder
and my head abruptly hit the bricks
they thought it was hilarious
but i didn't
all eyes were on me
i marched away

far away

you had a look in your eyes
they said
in later years
you weren't fully present

limbo

maybe i wasn't
always present with them
in the world of
the living
because my depression
was causing me
to slip more towards
the world of the dead

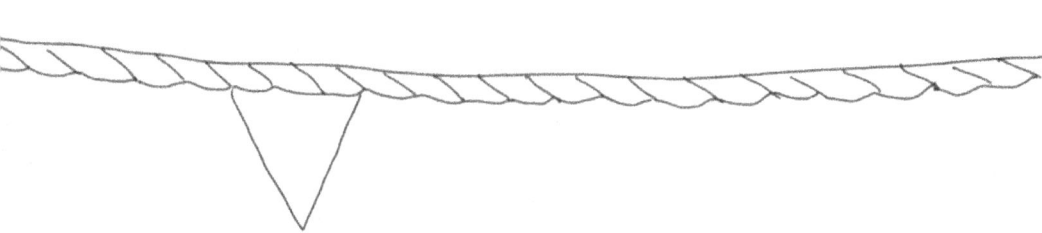

13 years old

i stood outside the library
quickly eating my lunch
when one of my teachers
approached me
holding my shoulder gently
are you alright? she asked
i smiled weakly
yes i said
just waiting for a friend
she nodded to me saying
*ah i see. well i'll see you
in class, take care of yourself*
and walked downstairs
she didn't realise that
what i really meant was
i'm waiting for someone
to be my friend

hallway

that hallway has watched many heartbroken
people cautiously walk through it

absence note

my teacher kept observing me
because i was so detached
from everything going on
around me
the class content
the people
myself
he just kept looking at me
with sorrow in his eyes
and when my appointment
with the school counsellor
came around
i gave him the note quickly
so he wouldn't keep me behind
to talk
but he tried to
are you okay? he asked
with increasing concern in his tone
i held back tears
yes i said blankly
and left

bus route

i didn't want
to get off the bus
i wanted it to
travel forever

glass wall

why do you all have to be out there
sitting at tables laughing, smiling
going out for dinner or taking road trips
plastering photos on social media
talking so casually about it
why
why do you have it all
why is your whole week always
booked out as if you're exclusive?
what's your secret?
i want to know what it's like
for people to see me
instead of me waiting for them
everyone stop smiling and laughing
or i will tear
myself
apart

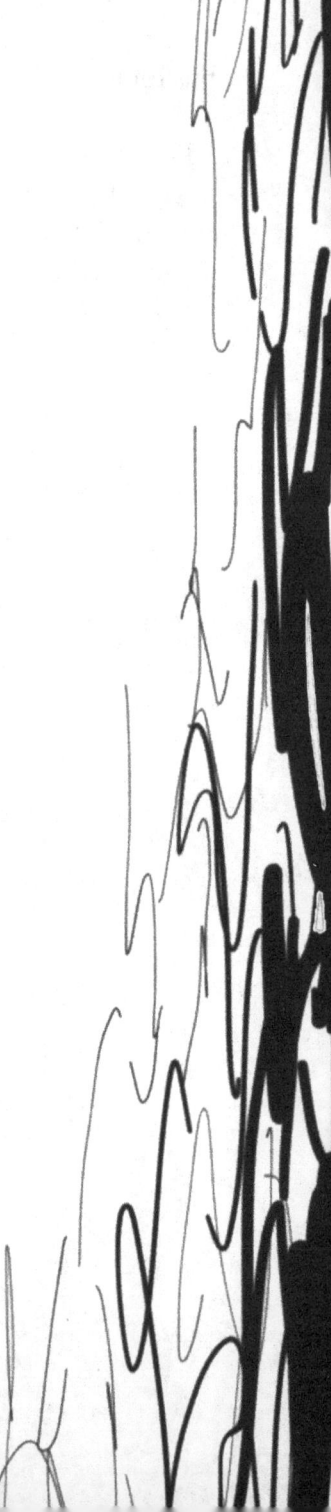

ella zelensky

choking

i'm mumbling gibberish
tears falling in streaks
down my face
i'm fumbling for
the right words
to express my feelings
but i'm crumbling, swaying
and when you step back a bit
i start falling to my knees
my sparkling eyes staring
straight at the sky
as i choke thinking
i am the only one
who knows what my own thoughts are

lifeless

it is a
painful thing
to feel
as though one
with the inanimate

jewellery box

i cannot sparkle
or twirl beautifully
forever

divine decree

disco light

we are so little
little, little beings
flying and flowing in
different directions
from a distance
it is a beautiful
yet lifeless looking
dance
a slow disco light
tired and enrapturing
shifting round
a conflicted romance
its illumination is clever
at making what's cold
appear warm, beautiful
and timeless
though we are finite

ella zelensky

explosion

sometimes years of
holding something in
brews emotions that
will inevitably throw
glass shards
in everyone's direction
without the person
ever meaning to
hurt anybody

someone

i wanted to be held
in someone's arms
they didn't necessarily
have to understand
what was going on
but i just felt like i
needed to be protected
to breathe in time with them

divine decree

violence

depression
is entering
a room
devastated
by violence

ringing teachers

i did skip classes
i did skip assembly
i wasn't late to school
i was holding my mouth shut
in the girls' bathrooms
i was holding my mouth shut
so my faltering voice
wouldn't echo
loud enough for the girls
entering and exiting
to know i was in there
that i existed
i'm sorry that you got
concerned
i was too

to exist

sad experiences exist
people themselves exist

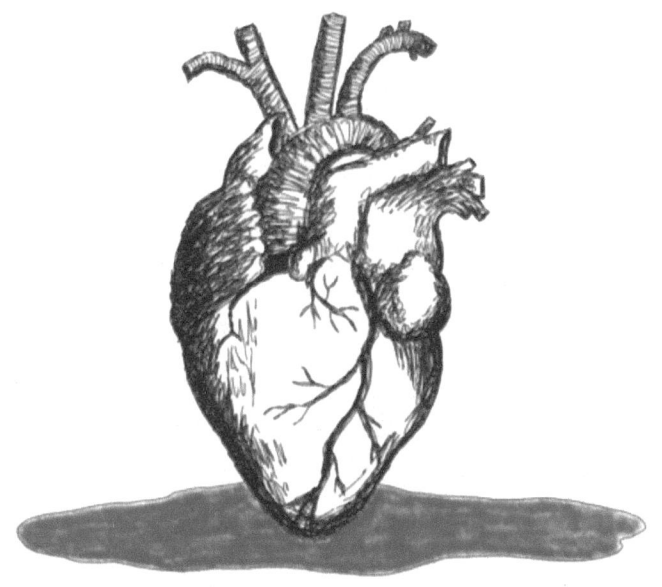

intrusive

i couldn't stop
thinking of not
thinking anymore

kind heart

you have a very kind heart he said
you treat everyone with
gentleness and kindness
you are a good person
i smiled to him and thanked him
can i hug you? he asked
the people around me
kind of paid attention to this
because they didn't want to
be hugged by or associated with
a boy who had a condition
but i said *yes*
his hug was beautiful
it was real and rare
full of love

teacup

my heart has broken
barely the sound
of a glass clinking
or a note on the piano
quiet
cautious
but ready

statue

i eventually turned still

class quiz

as i waited through classes
i tried to simultaneously
place myself in a separate
setting
one without people
or desks
or assignments
i walked alone
in a beautiful open space
with soft swaying grass
a field dotted with sleepy
bundles of flowers
laying beneath a rose sky
clouds of crisp definition
made way for the sun
and i stood still before it
this was my little wonderland
my teacher stared at me as
i paid more attention to my
internal reality than my external one
they looked as worried as i felt
but i decided staying in my
wonderland would save me
more than my marks
for our class quiz that week

ella zelensky

sign language book

the memory of him teaching me the signs
for the colours of the rainbow
as the evening sun illuminated
our happy, innocent eyes

therapy

sometimes i wish for rain

divine decree

attentiveness

there was little time
in your face
and reason in
your eyes
little detail
from your lips
and knowing
in your goodbyes

escape

i would awaken
like a flower
in the reversal of
its wilting
fragile, dazed
stare at the window
with distraught eyes
and return to
my pillow
my only friend

rest

lunch breaks and
weekends weren't enough

to be chosen

i wanted someone
to congratulate me
to vote for me
to be sincere when
they said
i'll vote for you
but i knew it
would never happen
for how could a
quiet girl with
unusual hobbies
and worldviews ever
be chosen as a
leader

applause

the girls who made vlogs
received applause
the girls who were
popular received applause
everyone received
applause
but when my film came up
not one person applauded
and it's absolutely
upsetting
that i already knew
they wouldn't

ella zelensky

never be the reason

i remember the days where people would
suspiciously go off in pairs until
the whole group had left me by myself
when people threw food at me that
used to be able to kill me
who would laugh at me as i
collected their test papers
or push me into the wall knowing
saying something back wouldn't help me
people who glared and sneered at me when
i walked into the classroom
the years when i would stand in a stall
in the girls' bathrooms crying my heart out
every morning tea and lunch
no one should ever be the reason
someone else didn't want to live anymore
i've given the insight
now it's time for change

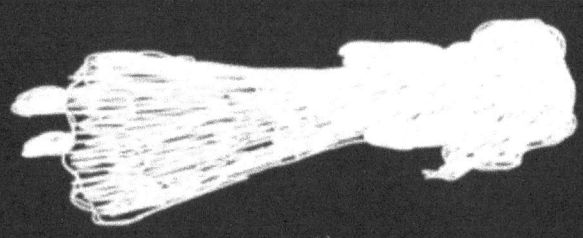

cater

i live
to serve others
so much that
i even make sure
the breaking
of my own heart
does not
inconvenience them

hold the door

the only thing that kept me
from crying out my anger
in front of some of those girls
in my classes was remembering
what they must be
going through too
so please
please go first
my heart said
i'll hold the door open
again for you

avoidance

they stayed away
from me
like i had
an illness

seizure

half of my vision
was consumed by
rainbow stars
my teacher
was blurred out
she was trying
to explain the task but
i only heard gibberish
what is happening to me?
i turned to my friend
but i couldn't understand
her or my own thoughts
my lips felt defeated
my limbs weakened
i was in panic
trapped inside
my own body

divine decree

water

water is beautiful
in moments of
confusion and hurt
its pouring
the way it dances
twirls
flows
how it falls
an elegance
an art
something we
reach to
and are attracted to
when troubled

osaka airport

*do you need someone
to help you navigate
the airport?* the lady
at the luggage check-in asked me
no, we will be fine i said
okay. just sign here she said
but as i began trying
to write my signature
my hand slanted down
the pen twisted in difficulty
and i managed only
a trembling line
the lady was talking with
one of her friends as i briefly
glanced to her in fear
and my heart sunk
i frowned after realising
i couldn't write my signature
as i used to

ella zelensky

mute

press your concerned fingertips
to my chest, and you will hear
chimes and marbles shivering
touch my lips and you will feel
words i have kept for longer
than both our lives combined
but if you reach for my eyes longingly
my focus will slide
so guide me gently
gently back to rest
for you have now felt what i feel
sit with me where we poured
beautiful, silent water

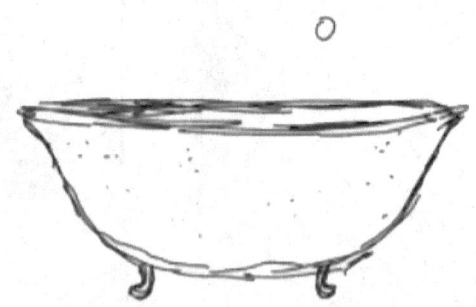

cut off

i shared the same birthday
as someone else
we made a cake
to celebrate
and as everyone was
singing happy birthday to us
one of the girls recorded
a video of the moment
but made sure to
cut me out of the video
as uploading a video that
featured me seemed to be
detrimental to her reputation
in front of her friends
the *look* we gave each other
i won't ever forget

fear

i am not ready
for my own self

psychosis

when i was 4 years old
i thought my lamp was
dragging me back to my room
by the feet and killing me
i asked my parents
to take it away because
i couldn't tell the difference
between dreams and reality
when i was 18 years old
i thought my lamp was
watching me so it could
gather other objects and
hurt me when i was alone
i asked dad to take it away because
i couldn't tell the difference
between hallucinations and reality

glitch

the teddy bear was
playing games with me
moving its head
when i did
laughing as i
tried to prove to people
that it was glitching
back into position

ella zelensky

auditory hallucination

the garage door creaked open
and i heard the car park
dad said *hey, i'm home!*
opened the back of the car
and took out grocery bags
when you're ready, can you
help me bring these inside?
yes i said, *just let me finish*
this last sentence of my essay
the first of the grocery bags
he brought in contained what
sounded like cans
probably diced tomato or corn
i thought
next came bottles of juice or milk
okay, i'm coming i said
i walked outside happily to the car
but the door to the garage was shut
i opened it
the car was not there
i turned in panic to
the kitchen bench
no bags
my eyes widened in fear
as i could hear those soft sirens
going off again
the hallucination was
laughing at me

ella zelensky

paranoia

cups, bowls, books
they were all alive
recording my every move
they were staring at me
without any eyes
jump scaring me
and i couldn't stop
looking at them in fear
they're going to
follow me i thought
and when i ran away
i had to make sure
they weren't

shriek

i was closing the bathroom door
but some girl started
whispering to me
i paused
tried listening to her
but couldn't figure out
what she was saying
she sounded distressed
when i continued to close
the door until it was shut
she shrieked my head into a spin
like girls do in horror movies
don't leave me! she screeched
don't leave me don't leave me
don't leave me don't leave me
i slammed the door shut

swapped

shoulders
left and right
switched positions
their imaginary locations
and shapes
buzzing convincingly
in the air above my lap
legs and arms
longer, then shorter
what age in my life
were they mimicking
my hands felt
childlike, small
my face
didn't feel like
mine either

zombies

someone hit the wall
i thought it was an accident
tried going back to sleep
but someone else
thumped the wall
and another
and another
5, 10, a whole crowd
they were *desperate*
they were searching for *me*
stacking themselves until
my bedroom wall would collapse
i pulled the sheets over my ears
praying until their screeching
died down softly

jamais vu

i came to school
and felt like i'd never
been there for the
4 years i had been
it was creepy
it was distressing
i caved into myself
until my limbs went numb
cancelled my exam and went home

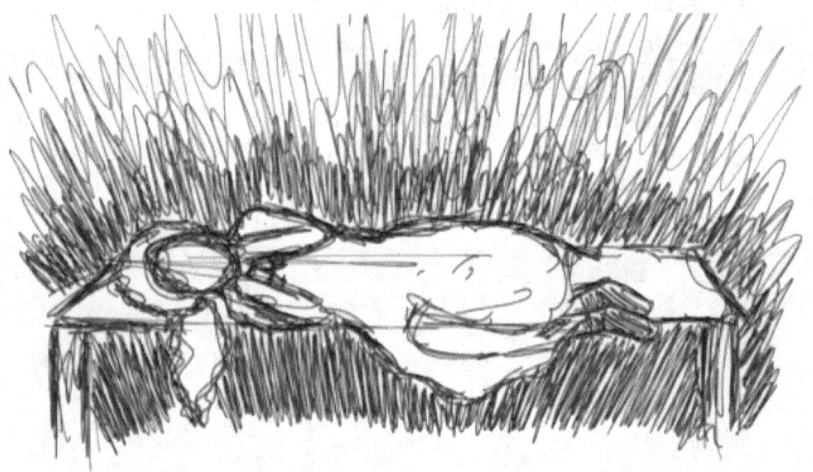

adulthood

these things
and places
i was fearing
were not things
or places
a kid should
have feared
into their adulthood

divine decree

stars

after learning about
vincent van gogh's
medical history
it is no wonder he
depicted the starry night
the way he did
i see his work differently now
the sky looks like
auras made pretty
and hallucinations that echo
and rivet and curdle
i have never related
to a piece of artwork
more than this
i feel his pain
but commend him for
the way he beautified it

be considerate

i had anaphylaxis to egg for 17 years, and it truly was a struggle. when you mention anaphylaxis to people who don't have it, the first and potentially only image that comes to mind for them is the food you miss out on. but it was more than that. missing out on food definitely hurt, but it was the social aspect of it which got to me more.

because my allergy was life threatening, and because what i was allergic to was basically in everything, everywhere, my ability to go out with people was limited. i couldn't have cake, cupcakes, biscuits, slices, brownies, cookies, pies, donuts, certain types of ice creams, ice cream cones, waffles, pancakes, pizza, pasta, certain chocolates and milkshakes, crumbed chicken, battered fish, salads, noodles, dumplings, burgers and more at almost every restaurant there was. even if a particular ice cream flavour had no egg in it at all. if mum asked the person behind the counter if they used the same scoop for the rest of them, and they said yes. it meant everything was cancelled.

my heart sunk when i would stand quietly, fearfully, in the corner as the other kids picked whatever they wanted. not only this, but they could stand in a circle. laugh. sit down, even. and help themselves to more. i couldn't have more, because when i asked them if i could pick first for the sake of my safety, they didn't care.

they still cross-contaminated everything. every crumb that fell on the floor we had to sit on for lunch. every door handle they twisted. every whiteboard marker they held and tried to pass on to me. every desk lid they touched. ruler. stack of assessment booklets. it scared me. but people didn't care. and if they did care, they couldn't fully understand.

now, i don't have this allergy anymore. but it was replaced by a different condition. just when i had finally caught up to the stage those around me were at in terms of their food and social independence, my new condition froze me in place. once more, everyone moved ahead with their cars, jobs, social lives, romantic partners even. i felt gutted. i *feel* gutted. and there is something awful that continues to shock me. the behaviour people demonstrated when we were kids. waving things in my face. laughing at me. leaving me out. it hasn't stopped. grown adults are doing the very same thing. they tell me the hundreds of dollars they've earned. show me pictures of their day out and ask me, very unnecessarily, to re-confirm to them how great it looked. they send me dozens of pictures of the car they bought.

and when i finally break. snap in half. shed a tear. stand up for myself. they get angry. make you feel awful for your reaction. this is what i say to those who have done this to me. *i have lived 20 years behind glass.* watching others claim that work hard pays off, because their hard work - very luckily for them - paid. off.

be considerate

but mine never did. everything i did was torn to shreds in front of my eyes. whilst the other kids sat back and laughed, i was *screaming* inside. screaming because the girls who bullied me got captain roles at school. academic badges. friends. boyfriends. and no illness.

i can feel myself sitting on a single chair. watching the years pass. there are tears in my eyes. "it feels painful because," i say. and i can see in their eyes an emptiness. an absence of understanding. a squinting of the eyes. "i don't get it, so i'll hurt you," it feels like their actions are saying.

now, in this book, i am standing up for myself. if i gave you the isolation that i had and have now. transferred my pain. let it course through your body. and then wave my privileges in front of you. saying *look at this, look at that*. and then you cry. if i got my foot and pinned you to the ground as you were sobbing. telling you to swallow your attempts at setting the boundary. or why you're hurting. would you be angry too?

for the sake of the heart of a human being. remember your intuitive capacities. see beyond yourself. stop dishing out the pictures. hold their hand instead. kiss them on the cheek.

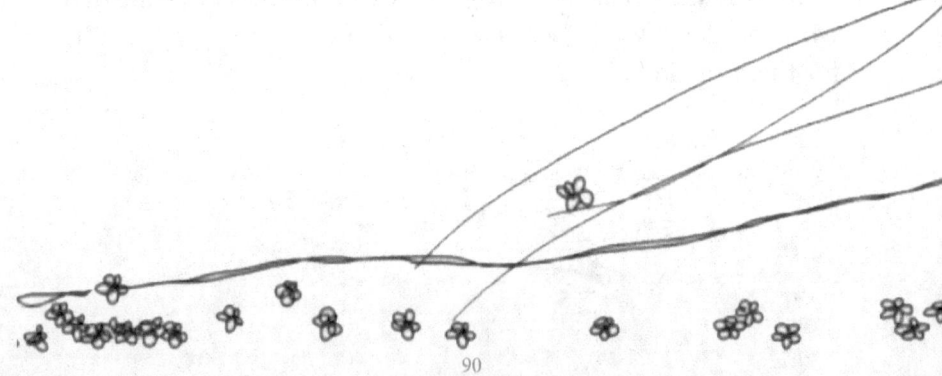

ella zelensky

not sure

sometimes i feel
that my hallucinations
are less frightening
than not knowing
what is real in
my friendships

radiate

the sun was waiting for her
to say hello to them as she did
each morning atop the mountain
this was routine
a connection they had
but she didn't make an appearance
for weeks
the sun grew concerned
sending its rays
on a lookout for her
search for my lovely companion
the sun said
tell her how honoured i am to cast
my light upon her beautiful face

divine decree

end of the day

a room darkened
by night -
my solace,
when all else fails

done

i was so done
with trying to
stay afloat
that i just
let life
throw me at
its walls

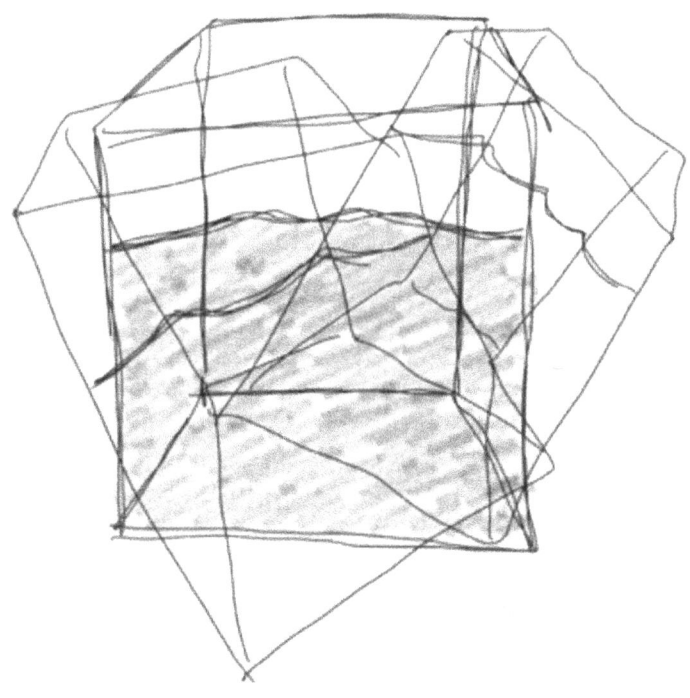

the end of year 12

maybe they went silent
after i became unwell because
they realised they should have
been kinder
it was truly silent
in that classroom
truly silent

upset

the lakes will swirl
and the rivers will flood
and the seas will rise
and rise and rise
from the pain my
heart carries
until they begin
making their way
to the weeping call
my soul echoes
on a global level
and it will cocoon me
returning me to
my child form
before you can ever
come near me again

conquering the enemy

i stare the enemy
straight in the eye
as it entices me
to surrender
am i the ender
of it or me

to stay

telling someone
to leave
is sometimes
one of the most
powerful and
contradictory ways
of internally asking
for someone
to stay

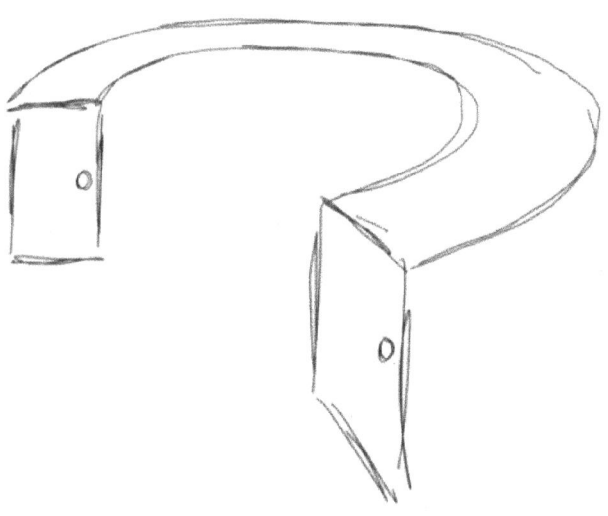

divine decree

creatures

like ink
i've let spill
threatening
creatures
i cannot kill

ella zelensky

divine decree

ignorance

to see someone
immersed in water
convulsing for
oxygen
yet telling them
to hold their breath
for longer

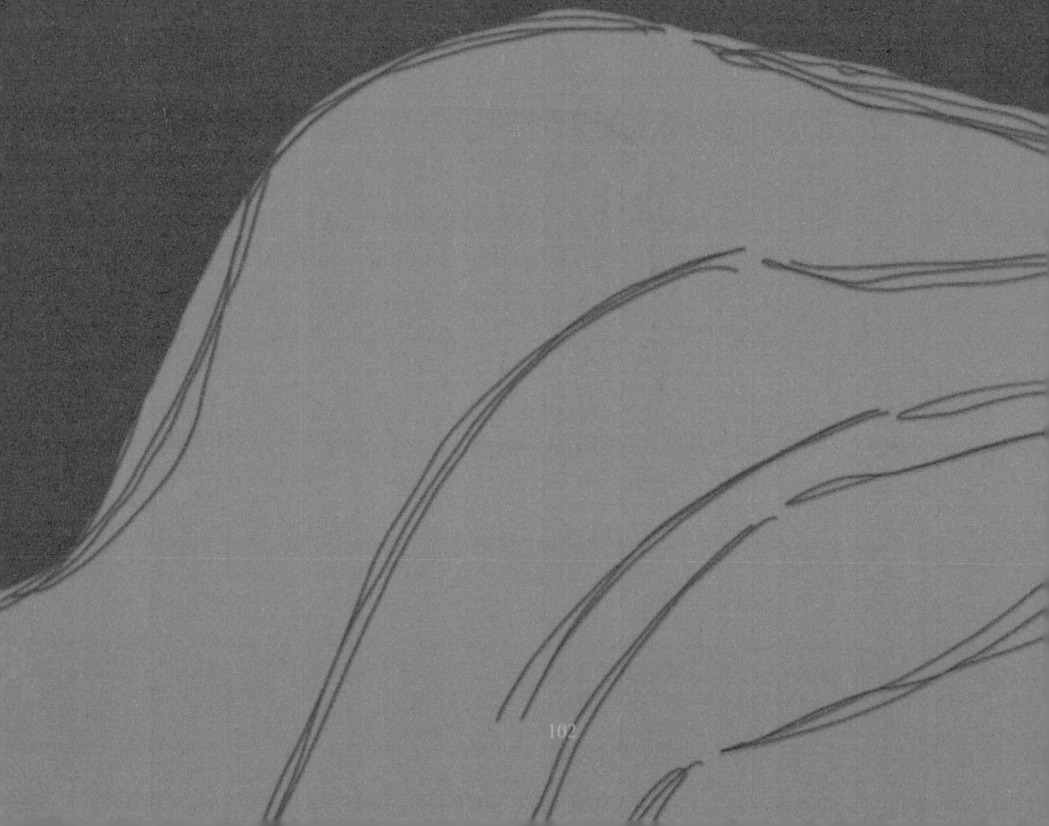

ella zelensky

catch

they threw something
i couldn't catch

expectations

they say it's no big deal
until they hit their brick wall
by then i'll stand back and say
now you stand tall

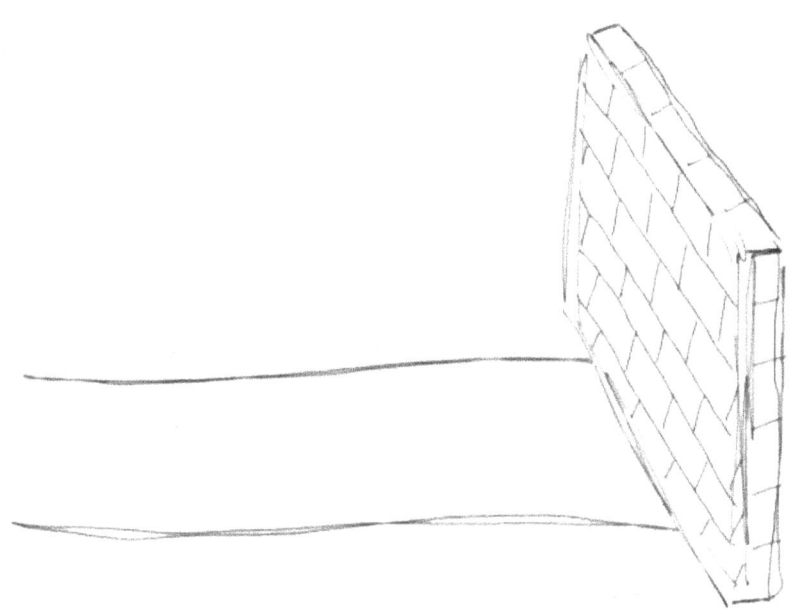

distress

it's always being fuelled
just as i hush the fire
and have it settle
another form of pain
is thrown its way
and the fire wakes
up again like a
startled, upset child
it cries again and again
arms outstretched
body convulsing in flames
and i try to hush the child
but the child
won't sleep
the child is sleepless
the child is i

underwater ballet

this water will
kill her soon
but she keeps going
without really
knowing
or maybe she knows
little oxygen
and she still glows

association

did they finally start
to treat me well
because i became
a university student
because i was the sister
of my popular brother
or because they loved
who i was
you can't just treat me
like i don't exist one minute
and then try to convince people
you have an association
with me the next

give, always

life beat me up
for being kind
but i kept my hand
up
it kicked me to
my knees
and my hand
trembled down
a little
but after years
of this brutality
i shook
back onto
my feet
stared my
purpose
right in the eyes
once more
and
kept
my hand
up

new day

i tell myself
i won't wake up
tomorrow
but end up
doing just that

the key

how did it
never occur to me
that my adversities
were the key
to my destination

affirmation letter

after graduating year 12, i finally had the chance to read all the affirmation letters people gave me. and i was amazed by something in particular - many people wrote that *my smile* made their day. that when i arrived at our group in the morning or passed by them in the hallway... even if just once... my smile changed everyone's mood. that my laughter picked everyone up. i honestly did not even know that my smile alone did that. even writing this now makes me cry because most of you knew what i was going through medically. you saw it all. you sat with me in sick bay. you saw me seeing stars. you saw my legs going weak. you saw me when i was having trouble talking or remembering. you saw me leave class early. and you were with me as i waited to be picked up halfway through school. you've literally held my hand through these times and i'm beyond grateful for that. these affirmation letters about my smile and laughter... i hadn't even realised that i was smiling and laughing *that much*. seriously. what i do know is that in that last year of high school, the smiles and laughs i do remember were genuine. i was happy despite what was going on. i would laugh until i couldn't breathe. i'd start laughing again in class after the joke finished 4 hours earlier (my close friends will understand this one). you knew how i was and how i still am - by this i mean me in my most happy and carefree form. i just want to say that i love that this is what you remember me by. i hope our friendship spans our lifetime. i love you all.

the coping

love
it was love
that kept me
going
like a firefly that
would meet me
every day
and guide me
forth
a little thing
it was
but a brave thing

leaving school

and when we graduated
i passed the bathrooms
i used to cry in
i passed the classrooms
i had sad memories in
the library i used to
hide in
and the *driveway*
i used to dread walking
because i was afraid
of my future
it was all over
i was leaving
i survived this place

willingness

i would rather
have gone through
that depression
for doing the
right thing
than doing nothing
at all

reversed progress

one day before
the end of year 7
a friend of mine said

    i want to be popular.

i tried to hide my frown
but told her

    okay

hoping that if she did
choose this life path
somewhere in her heart
her original, beautiful self
would at least stay

life beyond school

popularity
doesn't work
in the real world

leave

when you begin
to contemplate leaving
a fake group
they will advise
subtly that you
do not leave for
your sake
but simultaneously
for the sake of
fortifying their
own reputation
from widespread exposure

-     deciding for your sake threatens theirs

mistake

we chase false cures in circles
yet wonder why we ache
it's the absence of self confidence
that bears the said mistake

divine decree

undoing

undo yourself
of the system
and experience
love in its original
selfless form

"she's the one"

do not try to
get from girls
what you believe
you lack
i told him
you've told me
about the countless girls
you've dated
but when you ask
for my advice
and say you value it
you keep running back to
the same girls
in different girls
and cause more damage
for yourself

broken up

from the moment two
co-dependent people
have decided to
date each other
they have immediately
and simultaneously
broken up

confession

she went to the bathroom
buzzing with a cocktail of emotions
smiling, beginning to frown though
she slammed her hands
on the edges of the basin
and stared right at her
curious eyes outlined in ink
he said he wants me
she laughed
sounds great
but she suddenly didn't
feel that great anymore
the music outside was pounding on
the bathroom walls so much that
she felt the space was shrinking
all the chatting outside
had no substance to it
the only substance it did have
was the effects of alcohol
she began crying in this little bathroom
i don't know if i want him she thought
i'm not happy here
i'm heartbroken here
someone save me

like versus love

i'm in love
this is love
we're in love
they say
but they're
mistaken
love is rare
you *like* that
boy or girl
but you don't
love them
there's a
crucial
difference
between
let's make each
other feel good
and
i'm enamoured
by your heart
and mind

periphery

when someone
keeps us distracted
by putting nice things
in front of our eyes
they will train
our focus to stay there
so that what they do
in our periphery is
blurred enough that
we don't notice
or if we do
we defend its vagueness

making moves

desperate words through
desperate advances
i watch in fascination
their curious dances

'attractive' traits

it is outrageous
that many boys are
dating the girls
who bullied people
to the point of depression
how can you want
to live your life
with someone
who made someone else
not want
to live theirs

crumble

he will make love
with insecurity
and enter a marriage
of scarce security

player

don't get up
all of a sudden
and introduce
yourself to me
with a smirk
when your
girlfriend showed
up an hour later
let me make it clear
i'm not interested
in men like you
and you're not
the king you
think you are

divine decree

to leave

i hope she finds someone
beautiful instead
someone who doesn't
chat up other girls
behind her back
when her heart believes
you are her other half

failed attempt

you raised an eyebrow
wondering why i didn't
drool for you like
the other girls did
you see
the difference here
is that i am proud
of the young woman
i have become
it is contentment with
oneself that decreases
a desire for the other
you can flirt with me
all you want
but it will never win
over a happy heart
and i think that that
is a beautiful thing

speak up

i confront when necessary
but there is a difference
between feeling threatened
and feeling afraid of
being enlightened

get ready

do not think
that your actions
come without
consequence
do not count
on the fact that
i will say nothing
i may keep quiet
but nature's way
will not

divine decree

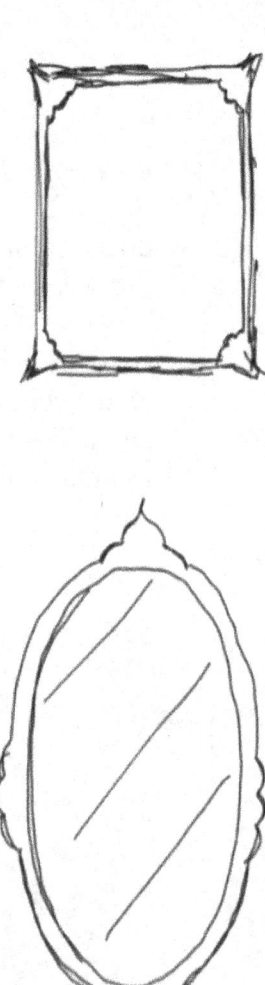

museum

i walked through
the party
surrounded by a display
of sexuality
one of the boys
eyed me
halfway through
kissing a girl
as if he wanted
to switch from
her to me
or enjoy us both
but i told him
to back off
this was a party
but its behaviours
were nothing
worth celebrating

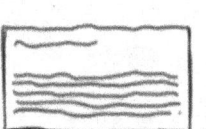

ideal

*she's so hot
every guy in town
is after her
her body is amazing
she's popular
with everyone
she's every
bloke's dream
he said
if only you saw
how she bullied
me to tears
at school
i thought*

western "love"

living in the west
i've lived my whole life
seeing love being taken
as a joke
there are no
cultural love songs
no slow courtship
no profound or
sacred moments
living vicariously through
non-european
romance movies
has been the only way
i can pretend i belong
to a different life
and wish for
the deeper love
they succeeded
in valuing
but we in the west
failed to

eradication

it's no longer sacred now
this is the culture
we wanted to create

the truth

intimacy
a sacred thing
barely treated as such
it is more commonly known
by physical union
as we see with abundance
and even carelessness in society
but what of that which
is beyond action
what of soulful attraction
and an intellectual interaction
it is easy for two bodies
to seek one another's pleasure
but even rarer a thing
to find the more
profound treasure:
love

drug

i know it's wrong
he told me
but i can't help it
i just keep going
for those girls
it's like a drug

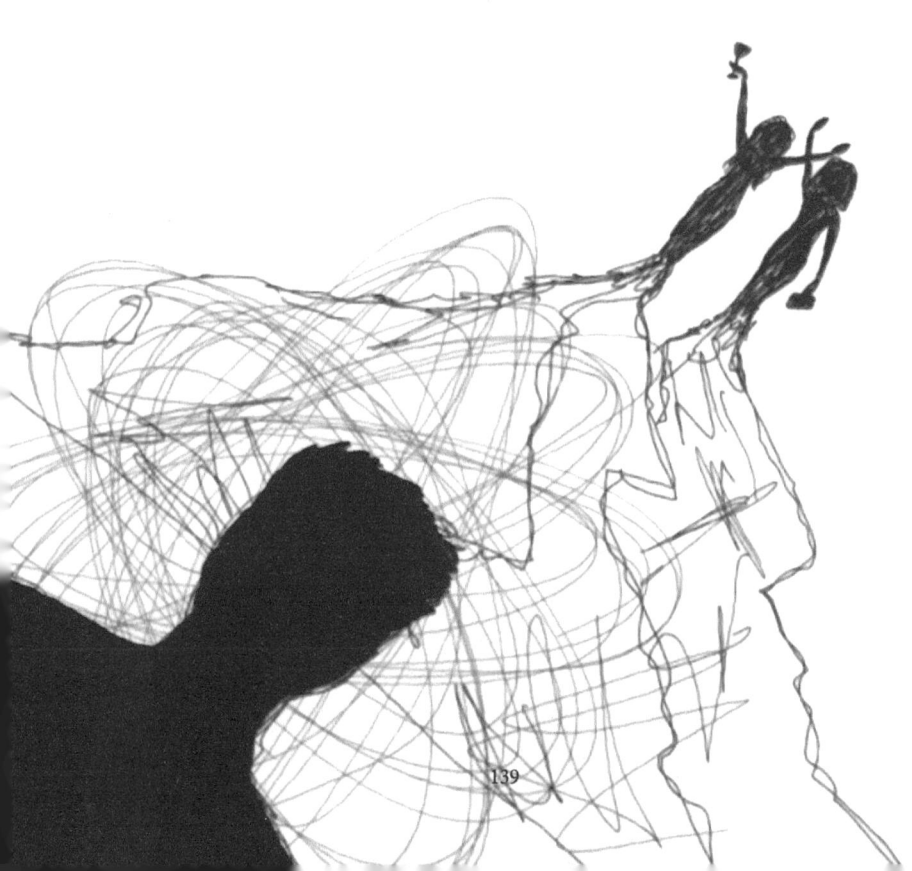

differentiate

do not confuse
certain passions
for others
it is crucial that
we can differentiate
between lust
and love

recognising

we will eventually know
what to search for
when we have seen
too much of
what we would not
when the crowd
becomes deafening
we cannot
hear ourselves

the right person

the right person will
enlighten you
they will keep
your eyes open
with mindfulness
and adoration
and not closed
in second thoughts

grievance

which of the two
do we have a habit
of grieving
the one who
was not right for us
or trying to be
the one who is
not right for us
how can we obtain
the right relationship
when we haven't
at the first level
with ourselves

discussion

the greatest
intellectual discussions
are when neither person
enters it to remain
unchanged

logic

it won't be fake
if you search for
something that isn't

mirror image

you will not find yourself
when getting with someone
who has also not
found themselves either
in the end
you will bring each other
closer to square one
than genuine happiness

lazy

keeping me within arm's reach
is the most subtle way
you can convince me to stay
close enough to maintain
my hope
but not too far away that you
inspire doubt within me
too quickly or easily

support

who will hold your hand
the whole way
ask yourself
and ask without fear
who truly cares for you

painful wait

one of the scariest things
is seeing an outcome
so intricately in the mind
that it cannot be
articulated by the lips
until it actually happens
and hurts someone

reckless

you have lost the
respect of your friends
because
you have lost respect
for yourself

false affirmation

instead of knowing where we really need to be
we chase people and situations that give us
a dose of excitement and surface level affirmation
this diverts us from the true source of happiness
we need, and we end up living in a cycle
of constantly returning to those surface level environments
identity thus becomes buried - unclear -
and our struggle only grows in reclaiming it

genuine friendship

enjoy someone's company
not their boosting of your
appearance

cure

people laugh at the child
born with a condition
while the mother
doesn't know if she
should cry or not
if only they knew that
their beautiful child was
about to change the world
don't cry over something
that isn't the case
your child is the cure
for our human race

mixed features

I send all my love to the mixed race
children all across the globe
who were told they were
too dark or whitewashed
who were excluded from
both of their own communities
who believed they were imposters
of their own races and cultures
who looked in the mirror
and took off cultural clothing because
others said they were imitating them
so much love needs to go to the children
who lived with confusion over their
beautifully ambiguous mixed features
the question of *who am i*
takes us years to answer, but
we are the evidence of increasing unity
in our world today

ella zelensky

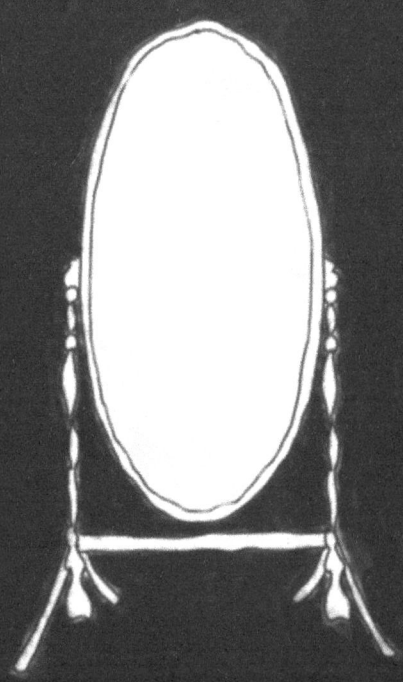

a change of mind

as i washed my face
quietly at the basin
i pulled my face towel down
to reveal my staring eyes
brown, with hints of green
mascara fading away gently
from the corners of my eyes
i began to see the exquisite
patterning of my olive skin
and realised *i liked myself
without makeup* far more
than with
i looked beautiful
honest
striking
real

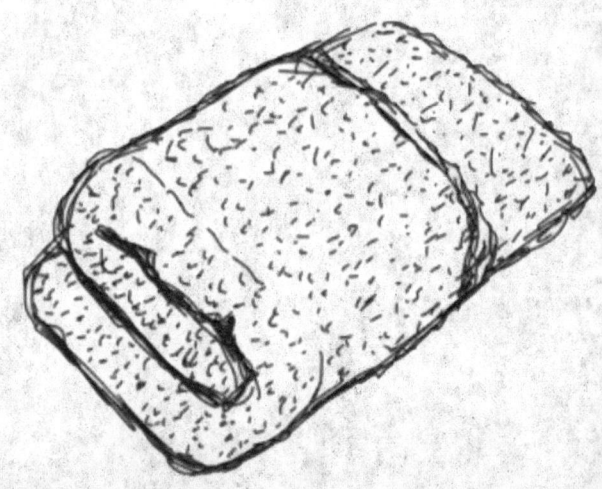

irony

we have made constant distress soothing
and an awareness for life's gifts
a threat to the internal system
we have built for ourselves -
in other words
we are protecting ourselves
with the threat itself

universal

you are someone
with rare traits
who is fighting
to make those
rare traits
universal traits
again

dismantling

it's rare because
we chose for it to be
we created this system ourselves
so we can dismantle it
kind hearts and free hearts
they don't have to be rare at all

it exists

you say i am waiting
for something that
doesn't exist
but you don't realise
that i've seen it before
in its purest form
it *lives*
it traverses the
very planet we live on
as we speak

both sides

i used to speak to my mother
about the people in school
who i thought didn't like me
or maybe they thought
i didn't like them
when all this time it could have
just been misunderstanding
had we initiated a conversation
all those years ago
a friendship may have formed
it seemed popularity scared both
sides into never considering it

the mind of a child

the kaleidoscope and
building blocks
return my mind to
my childhood where
we were taught to
treasure and follow
our imagination
it is disturbing to me
how quickly they ripped
that time from us
we were robbed of our
potential before we could
even learn how to write
sentences to
speak against it

you don't know how to write

you don't know
how to write
with structure
some of my teachers said
you need to learn
how to
but do i?
i thought
what will be
more beneficial
for me
getting good grades
or saying what
the world needs
to hear?
i'm prepared
to sacrifice the former
to live truly
with the latter

divine decree

convinced

i equated my worth
to the things
i decided
i would never have

assignments

it is not that
i don't care
about my assignments
i said
it is actually
a case of
me caring enough
about them
to fight for shifts
in education
even if i'm
the only one
taking the risk

abc or humanity?

i used to cry to my mother
in the car after school
about the grades i was
getting over and over again
not because i didn't get
grades a, b, or c
but because the messages
in my writing were
being rejected for years

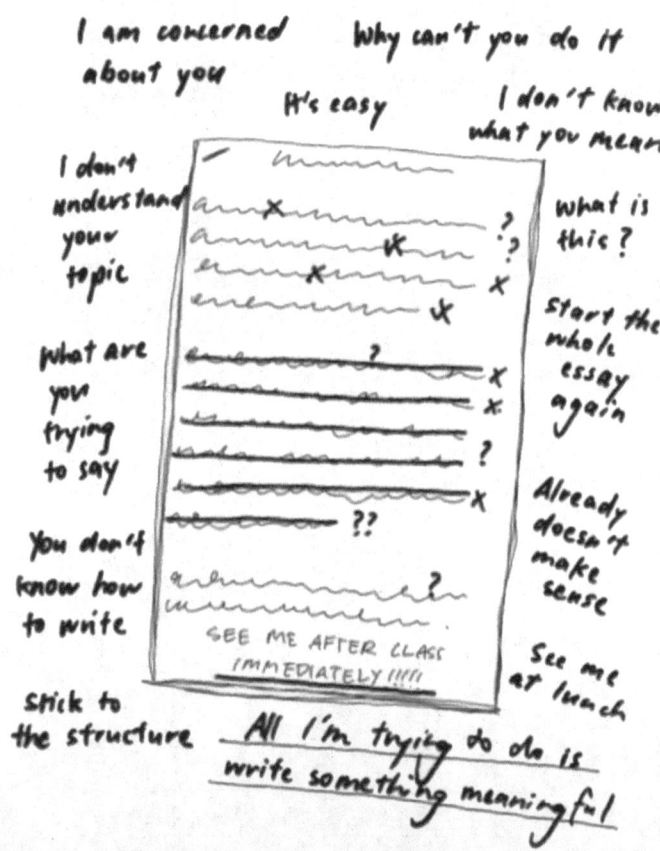

"strange mind"

unconventional
observation often
leads to a mind's
condemnation

cut-off

they could have been
standing at that podium
they could have been
on that researching team
they could have shown you
the even *bigger* ideas they had
if they qualified
for the next degree
they could have contributed
they could have changed the scene
they could have astonished you
but no
they're at *home now*
with their heads hung low
with all this incredible knowledge
trapped in their heads
that you never had
the chance to hear
don't ask for innovation or uniqueness
if all you do is grant the next stage
to an obedient selection of students
that's not how evolution works

valid contributions

to not be chosen is often a good thing
for we learn to maintain faith
and do so quietly -
it is not about the visual statement
of being elected for a position, but rather,
the beautiful efforts
behind the scenes

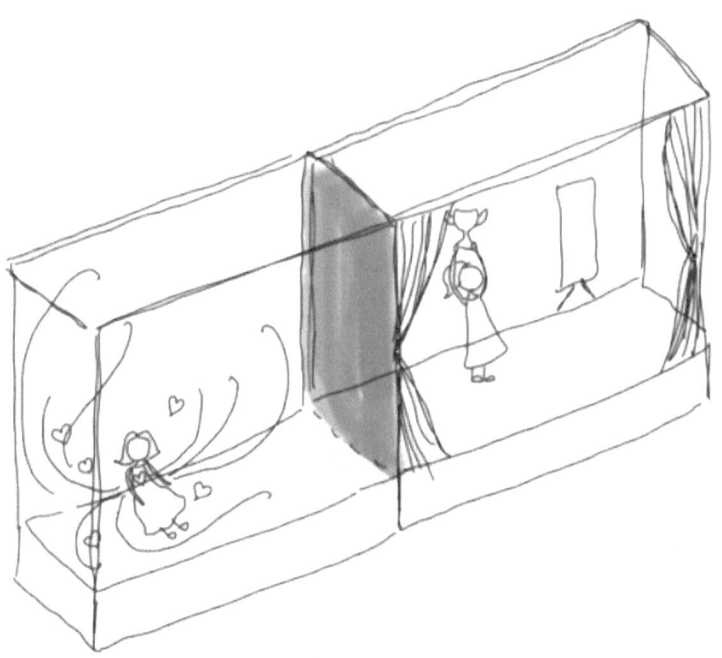

medical condition

and when i thought
my medical condition
was thrown my way
on purpose...
i realised it was.

it was thrown my way
as a gift.
now i am glad
i have it.

it humbled me.
and did not stop me
from where i
wanted to go in life.

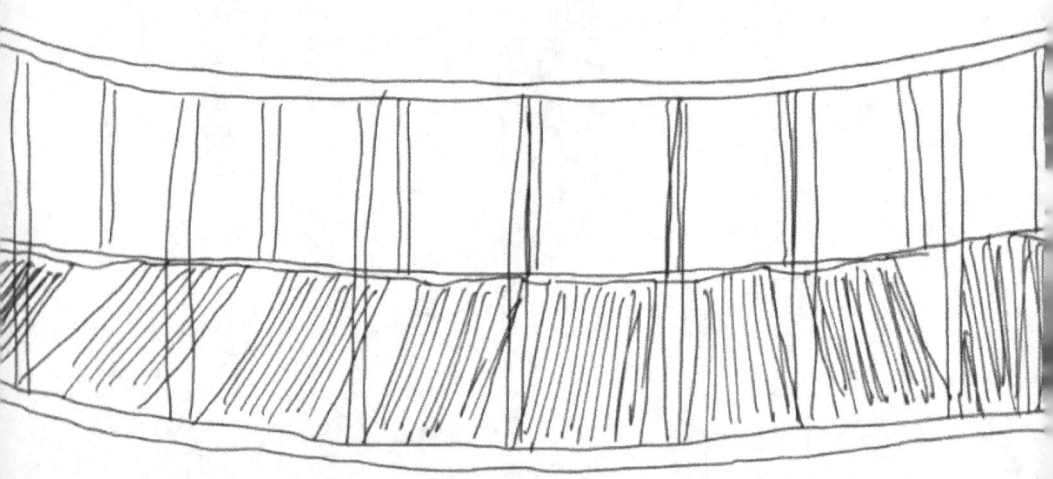

take that

what's funny now is that
the creativity i was
marked down for
in high school
is now the creativity
i'm getting unbelievable
marks for in university

academic award badges

my obsession
with academic badges
ended in high school
when it dawned on me
that academic badges
are awarded
if you demonstrate
you can be a robot
it made me realise
that i actually don't
want one at all
the real victory was
preserving myself
enough to
speak with originality
and challenge a system
in dire need of reform

the voice of potential

it is only now
two decades into my life
that i have come to wonder
how incredibly frustrated
my potential must be
to be raring to go
and yet i deny it
i banish it
because i'm so
awfully convinced
i can't do what i want to do

hourglass

i will only grow stronger
as the years pass
i'm not bound by
expectations or
the hourglass

"are you with it?"

it is funny
how i am
a multitude
of stages
beyond
where you
told me
i could ever be

divine decree

victory

i thought
it wouldn't end
but it did
i got through

song writing

singing seems to be
one of the only ways
men can let out
their emotions
without being judged

silent battle

no woman can argue
that men feel less pain
when men are the ones
who are taught
to never reveal it
do not dare mock them

male suicide

the boy walked
to the podium
in front of
my brother's school
one day
he said
i received news
that two of my
friends committed suicide
he paused to
take a breath
it seemed suicide
was all around me

two friends

two boys committed suicide
in my mum's high school
she said she could
remember their faces
how upset they looked
they weren't popular she recalled
the two boys were friends

murder

the girl was standing
next to her mother
in the kitchen
her father walked in
with a gun in hand
pointed it at her mum
and blew her head off
pieces of her mother
were everywhere
the ceiling
the walls
the floor
and the girl's face

-       a story from a girl my mother met at my age

exchange

*i inherited all
of their money
she said
and i'd give
it all away
to have my
mum back*

leap

and she hit the ground

too much

three girls
have attempted suicide
recently
by jumping off buildings
at their high school
one is on life support
this is a wakeup call

schoolyard | graveyard

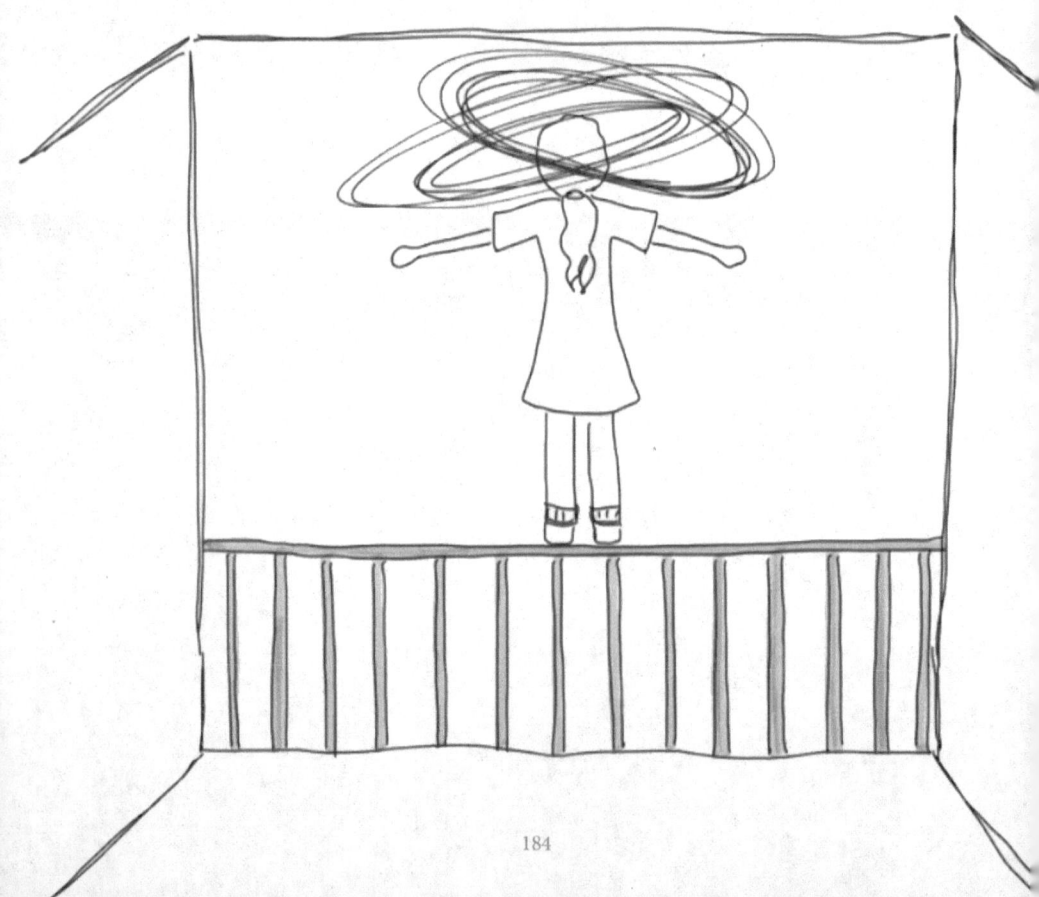

desperate

our generation is
killing itself
in any way it can find
we should be doing something

disappearance

we have all
walked past someone
who didn't intend
to be walked past
ever again

ever waiting

deeper conversations are dissipating
leaving old souls ever waiting

divine decree

save

you never know
whose life you may save

an end and a start

love is the beat
that revives the heart
and erases the end
that threatened a start

fearless compassion

compassion doesn't
have to be brave
it should be given
without hesitation

shaking hands

i will never forget
the days at the end
of high school
where girls would
one by one start
coming to me
to apologise
for it was not just me
who deserved an
apology for misunderstanding
someone
this was the greatest lesson
out of all my lessons
in high school

- i misunderstood them just as equally

the right friendships

one of the most unfortunate losses in friendships
is fearing ourselves and reputations enough
to let go of the friends who are actually
right for us

microphone

someone passed the
microphone
to you
you told me to rise
and i did, a little scared
of being in front of everyone
but you began speaking
saying
i just wanted to tell you
you are such a nice person
and i'm so sorry
if i've ever hurt you
i bowed my head to you
and quietly said *thank you*
but you must know
i was about to cry
when you said that

it's okay

you didn't
hurt me,
you know
i know you
think you did
but i promise
you haven't
i thought
it would be
important
to say it
in this book

motherhood

the day i become a mother
i vow to teach what will
educate the eyes
open the ears
and soften the heart
i vow to do all i can
to raise a child who
will help other children
and perhaps save a life

mother's eyes

when i was a child
i came home from school
and said to my mum
i wish i had
your blue eyes
because the people
around me had them too
living in a western country
was strange sometimes
but as an adult now
i realised
that i do have her eyes
different colour,
but the same shape
and not just this
but her motherly intuition
her creativity
it all comes from her
my mother's eyes

tatay ko (my father)

1971. manila, philippines. a baby boy is born. his mother loves him. his father abandons him after a few months. they suddenly belong to the streets.

1975. a black and white photograph. "to papa, do you still love me papa?" a bucket hat covering his little face. no message is returned.

but he survived his absence.

2002. brisbane, australia. a baby girl is born. her mother loves her. her father loves her.

2004. a baby boy is born, a brother. these are his very own children. he vows to provide for them what his own father could not for him.

2021. a father now for 19 years and counting. a survivor of his unforgiving past. victorious.

in every conversation he always makes sure to emphasise the importance of spending time together. reminding us to make wise choices.

and taking every opportunity to hug one another.

lola ko (my grandma)

a roaring in her system. a spark. a flip switch. people spat at her from all directions. this was nothing that could put out her fire.

we will *survive,* she thought.

not only a mother. a grandmother. this is all she needs to be happy.

sharp words. passionate purpose. gorgeous independence.

she didn't need what you didn't give anymore. and *that* she made clear.

lola, you were never here to quit. you and dad defied the odds.

lola, *you are my inspiration.*

this is the pain they have carried for decades.

this is the pain they have not vocalised once.

this is the pain unmet with remorse or apology.

this is the pain they were effectively told to swallow.

justice is well overdue.

it is only fair that their anguish finally be let out of their system.

this is more than a story - this is their right.

were they not human beings too?

ancestors

does my body remember
the lives of my
ancestors before me
my mother's father's side
who worked on
a farm they owned
or my father's mother's side
who worked on a farm
that owned them
does my body remember
their different countries
was i the mother of their
children with a different
mother tongue
how many children lived
how many children died
and how many were abandoned
why does my body pause
when ancestors are mentioned

vow

he told me
*i will be the father for you
that my father
never was for me*

spending time

parents are not
intruding on us
they are showing
their love
think about how
they must feel
when we dismiss them
one day
our door won't open
and we will wish
we gave them our
greatest love and attention
each time

recall

*you will understand
when you have
children of your own*
my parents say
i understand this now
it's not just about
paying the bills or
cooking dinner for us
it's about raising us right
it's about keeping us
safe from the abuse
of others and ourselves
it's about making sure
we stay close but allow
our child's independence
you will understand
their words whisper
in my mind as I cry
*when you have
children of
your own*

beloved mama

the child screams so hard
they hold their breath for too long
waiting anxiously for any helpers
to come along
pick me up, they cry
but take my mama with me too
the adults say *I'm sorry child*
there's nothing we can do
now it's just you

the rows of children

and the traumatised father
fell down to his knees
sobbing please
grant these precious
children ease

drowned

the ocean held
the boy in its arms
rocked him to sleep
as his mother would
and carried
him to land
saying here
take this boy
take his body
to the police waiting
at the shore
allow him to rest
and honour his dreams
by honouring the
safety of his people

(in honour of alan kurdi)

white noise

his irises swirl slowly
greyscale and lonely
an extensive white noise
he has much to tell
but too much trauma
to let it be known vocally
so he remains a memory
a boy that simply stands

eyelashes

grave were
the toddler's eyes
they carried
whole scenes
of violence and silence
their beautiful
long eyelashes
weren't thick enough to
catch the vulnerability
that leaked from them
every single trauma
revealed itself
in their eyes

ella zelensky

warriors

children killed in
war torn countries
are the warriors
we could not be

repeating memory

mama! papa!
and their faces
turn grey
time no longer
passes
each day
is that day

orphanage

she walked up
to the orphanage
gazed at the place
for a while
swaying slightly
distracted in her
vision of a future there
before her senses
reminded her
of her son cuddling her
in her arms
so young
and in need
in need of love
she chose him
over the orphanage

bias

one cue and we pounce as though a snake
so it must be that they are bad people?
yes is all we want to hear
for no will significantly shame our ego
how humiliating to perpetuate such pride
how embarrassing to intentionally dodge
an opportunity for growth

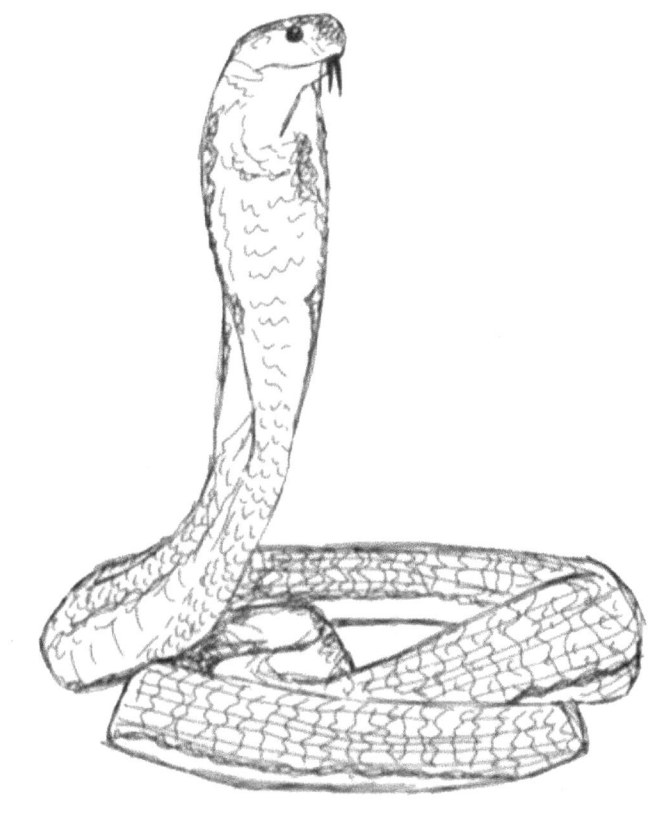

the death of the silenced

they have been pounding
their knuckles bloody
from beneath the ice
for so long
begging that someone
will notice them
before the frozen river
melts
and their dead bodies
fill and sway disturbingly
in the water

heartless

our lack of care
for the saving
of our world
is synonymous
with advocating
death

overexposed

by the end
of all this
they will no longer
have eyes

chance

how is it that when
we can clearly see
someone is being oppressed
or abused
we stand there and
don't challenge the oppressor
this person's life is
in our hands
but we end up letting
the person holding
so desperately onto our hands
slip from them

eternally

you will never make
us violent
it is what you
want to see
and want others
to see
and want us
to see
but it will not happen
for love overpowers
violence
even if violence reigns
for years

outcast

a 'monster' sad in face
but longing in its eyes
afraid of any kindness
and familiar with goodbyes

qualification

never say that someone doesn't
qualify for your community
if they aren't light enough
dark enough
or both
if they can't speak
the language
if they don't know
how to cook your food
if they don't participate
as much in your culture
if we can say you're a part
of our community
it is questionable to say
we're not a part of yours

interracial parents

growing up with
interracial parents
i learnt to see
them as mum and dad
instead of this colour
and that colour

protests

you will see us lead
with a flag in our hands
we refuse to fall dead
until the world understands

the realm of souls

i feel like i have met you before
a woman wearing niqab said to me
my heart froze
i was struck with fascination
i'm not sure i said, even though
i knew we physically never had.
that's funny. it really feels like
i know you from somewhere
she said.
we stared into each other's eyes,
trying to pinpoint this mysterious
relationship.
perhaps i met you in the realm
of souls i said
some part of me wanted to cry,
but this meeting was so
exquisite and unusual all at once
that i couldn't figure out why

ascended

i knelt next to
all the flowers
they gasped
as i prayed to god
about a love
that was coursing
through me
it was this that
made the forest smile
the flowers swayed
together in joy
tree leaves applauded
and the fireflies ascended

wait for me

when the princess of the mountains
died in his arms
his tears caused the four seasons
to cycle and cascade
over deep and endless fields
and when he couldn't breathe
out of sadness
she said
i will return to you
in our next lifetime
just wait for me
search for me
the prince's eyes burned with
pooling water
but the princess stared at him dearly
do not cry she whispered
do not cry for someone
you will never lose

reunion

i often wonder
when and where
i will meet my love
when the thought
upsets my heart
too much
i remind myself that
we met once
and will therefore
meet again

we will know

i will know
and you will too
our souls
will not part ways
if the connection
is true

confirmation

she ran to the forest
and asked if he was
her soulmate
bioluminescence responded

to dare

to dare but not scare
the art of careful balance

masquerade

you act all
sophisticated
behind your mask
but if i could
take it off
linger just before
your lips
brush my fingertips
gently across
your face
you might drop it
accidentally
and show me
the full version
of who you truly are

true selves

those who are easier to get with will make the connection harder
those who are harder to get with will make the connection easier

courtship

and we will continue
to dance around
what we suspect
yet do not dare
to suspect more
exchanging alternative
phrasings still beautiful
in delivery
but borderline enough
to not scare ourselves
or the other
if only years of
hidden meanings
could finally be
made clear
love could finally
expand beyond mental
confines without fear

spinning

long ago
our souls
danced in
circles
around one
another
eyes closed
laughing
until our
spinning turned into
standing still
and we
became one

mysterious impact

you were soundless
but stopped me
soundless
but it felt as though
you had walked into
the room having come
from a previous century
and were to leave again
to a future one
i wanted to work it out
and couldn't
but the look in your eyes
it did something to
my soul
like you were telling my
subconscious something
that wouldn't reveal itself
until later in my life

ella zelensky

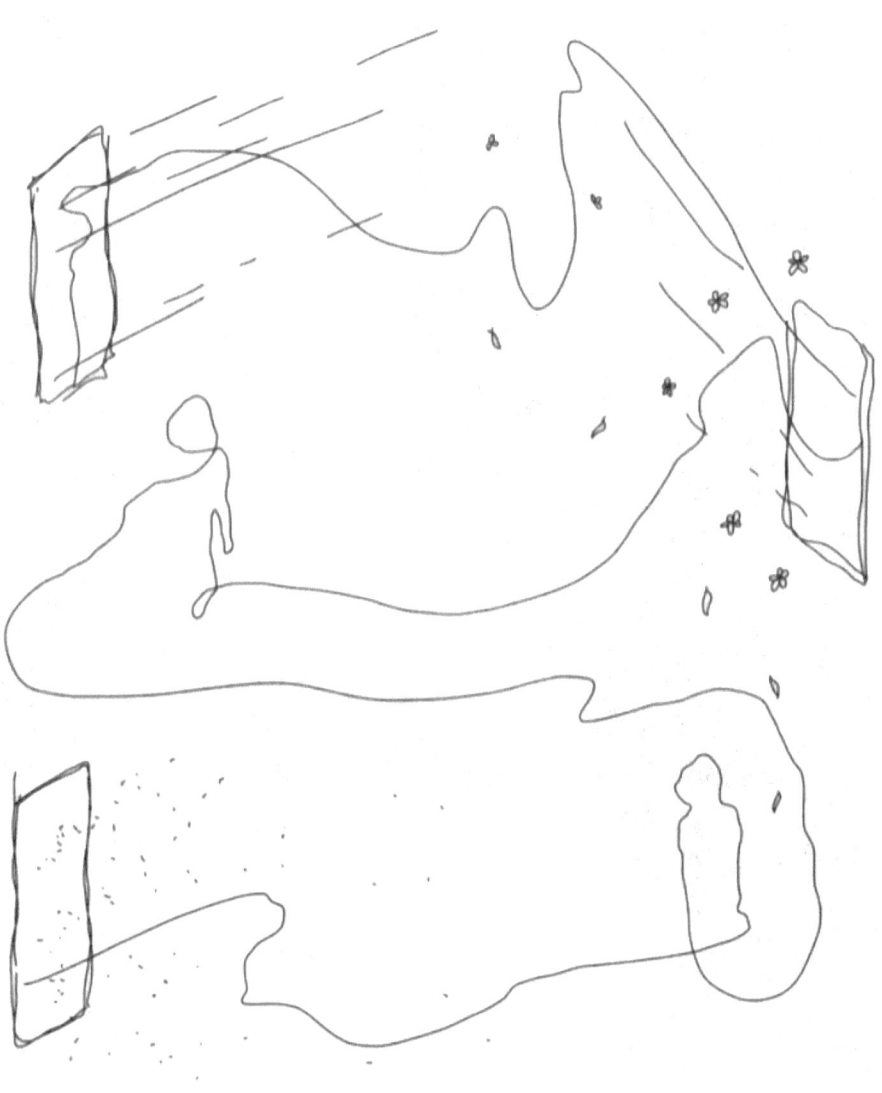

divine decree

garden maze

turning corners
for you

aching

where is my love
i ask god
i want to see
his eyes

eye contact

i think looking into the eyes
of someone i will come
to love will be intense
but intense with
admiration
intense with care

embrace

i would run to you

divine decree

to requite

it was her who awakened him
at the edge of his weariness
his pain she alleviated
as though he dropped
all his belongings
a gentleness cascaded from
her every movement
like water descending stairs
he feared not if she caught him
gazing longingly for her
perhaps it was right
for her to be made aware
but he would one day stand back
if his love was unrequited
this was only fair

(inspired by far from the madding crowd)

fear

he split in two
when she
did not love
him back
or perhaps her
falling into
the wrong love
was easier than
admitting her
affections
for the right one

effortless

an aurora flows between us

to yearn

it takes cycling through
the wrong people for many
to eventually realise
the type of person they
ignored in a sense
was actually the person
their soul cried for most

confession

if you love someone
do not delay in
your confession
it may be that they
twirl around to be
taken by another
and leave you
grieving something
they too may
have longed for

wide eyed

the unshakeable gaze
of a wide-eyed boy
falling in sincere love

changed

oh how beautiful
the girl
who changes
the boy
who swore
he could not
be changed

conflicted desire

it is difficult
when the heart
is asking for
two things
at once

message

not every emotion we feel
is a threat
let us not hold our ears
when an emotion
floats forth
and is saddened
by the fear of
its carrier

trusting

to catch me
in my gentleness,
they thought,
could never be done
for i will never reveal
to anyone
that my heart
can become
accessible by the love
of another

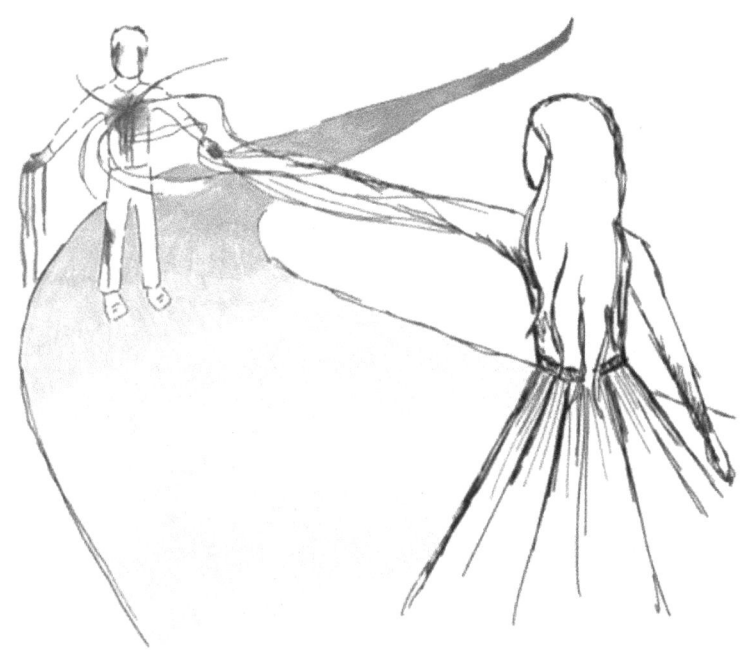

to trust

when we lock eyes
i tilt my head to the side
to examine your face
while you examine mine
i stand completely still
but i can feel our souls
departing our physical form
to touch hands
i've known you since
before we were born
i've seen your eyes before
we have loved before
i just need the courage
to follow where my soul
is drifting

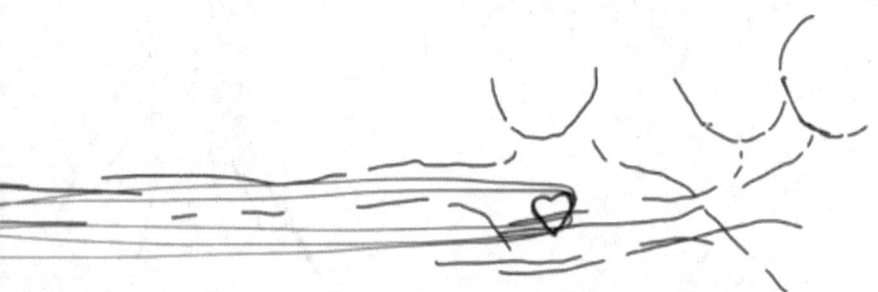

opposites

the balance
of opposite
traits continues
to and will remain
one of the most
beautiful phenomena
i will ever know

(inspired by the theory of everything)

i believed

for 17 years, i had no interest in god. i wasn't against any religions in any way either - it was just that i felt lost, and in a way settled with the idea of feeling lost. but many life events challenged me and my idea of god. as i've already shared in this book, i was bullied quite a lot in high school which lead to severe depression. being someone who always loved and stood up for others, as well as just being myself but getting bullied for it relentlessly was something i just couldn't understand or agree with. when i was then diagnosed with a neurological condition right in the middle of the year i was to graduate, it only fed my frustration and disapproval. my thoughts were: *how can god punish me this much after all the kindness i have given and struggles i have faced in my life? does god not know that i can only bear so much before i break?* my bitterness towards the nature of life was at its worst by the middle of year 12. i was feeling very conflicted and upset, not knowing how i could manage from that moment forth. one night i just burst into tears. i was lying in bed in the dark, and here's the contradiction: i was talking to god who i simultaneously didn't believe in. i was angry. *how could you do this to me?* i asked. *how much else do you think i can take? a god surely can't be like this. this is it. i don't believe in you anymore.* my teary eyes closed, and i fell asleep soon after. however. when i woke up the next morning, the most unforgettable moment of my life occurred. one thing i remember is that the light pouring into my room through the window shutters was golden. it poured into my room like a luminarium. and when i sat up, there was this strange thought in my head: *you believe in god.*

shock does not begin to describe the state i was in. it was strange because this thought - this decision - it wasn't one i had deliberately thought of or agreed to. it was just there. it was like it had been implanted into my head without me knowing. i felt like god had found me. i felt like my whole body was weightless, like my heart was reborn and happy. like i was being guided. every worry dissipated. this was my new beginning. my life since then has been absolutely incredible.

divine decree

the next chapter

and she gave herself to metamorphosis

ella zelensky

honesty

to say two things at once
and hope for both outcomes
simultaneously
will never give satisfaction
nor resolution
to the real and underlying
meaning we wish
to simply state

reaction

a collection of reactions
and the uncertainty of which

evolving

it is brave to let a past self die

the ability

falling out of arms
falling into air
falling to the floor
to catch me,
no one there
but the sunlight
caught my eyes
and they widened
holding tears
i've had the strength
to hold myself
and love
for all these years

trust

i planned
and planned
and my plans
did not reflect
any of my
hypotheticals
for god
knew what i needed
and surprised me
with what was
educational
humbling
and transformative

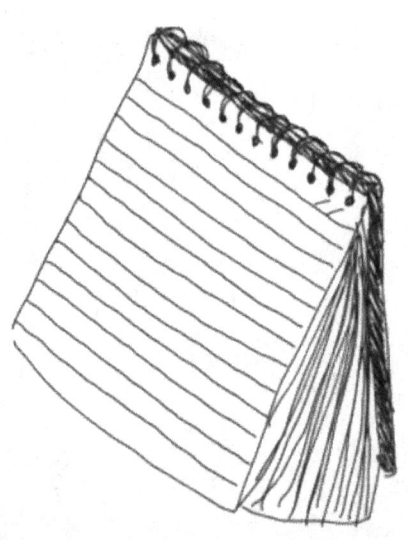

river

i am water
that follows
the predetermined path
of the river
which i know will
lead me
where i need
and am needed

quiet night

i don't mind not being able
to sleep at night sometimes
because it actually gives me extra time
to count and give thanks for my blessings

patience

a postponed blessing
isn't a cancelled one

prayer

prayer
has changed
my life

divine decree

these adversities that
i hated
did not come randomly
they were
necessary
they had meaning
all part of divine decree

finish line

my mouth gaped as i
saw the finish line
run they said
a smile on their face
you've made it
as i ran i waved
them goodbye
returning their smile
this is the moment
i once said i wouldn't see
but it was now the moment
i realised i was meant to be

afterword

wow. to know this is a book that people are holding in their hands is beyond incredible to me. this book was a difficult and daunting one to publish because it's an insight into what happened to me personally, and things that have happened to others. but i felt it was time to write it down. as much as this was a therapeutic process for me, i realised that it especially served as an educational tool to inform people that these experiences can and do happen. some people do, unfortunately, take their lives in circumstances like the ones i and others went through as detailed in this book, and a lot of us don't see more than the classroom appearance or the bus pickup in the afternoon of those who have left us. you and i have probably walked past someone who had no one to sit with. who was on their way to hide in the library or in a toilet stall. someone who was hurting. and even living their last day. these situations exist, and people themselves exist. i am so, so fortunate to have recovered from that time all on my own. because deep down i knew i didn't want to not be here anymore. rather, i wanted to change the 'here' a lot of us don't want to be in to a 'here' we love and savour. my dream to be a humanitarian worker largely comes from all the people i have met in my life, the struggles i have faced, as well as my familial heritage, hobbies, and academic studies. from the time we were pinning name cards to our shirts and learning the alphabet all the way to our adulthood. it always inspired this question for me: *why do people treat each other the way they do?* but more importantly: and *how can we fix it?*

About the Author

Ella is a mixed race Australian published author and current university student at the University of QLD, majoring in anthropology, and with interests also in Religion, Language, Cross Cultural Communication and Film and Television.

Since she was young, culture, race, religion, language, cinematography, and activism have played a significant role in her creative work and academic studies.

After struggling with fitting in during her early high school years, writing poetry helped her cope and rise above. Writing eventually became serious to her and she began sharing her work on her social media platform.

Ella published her first poetry book, Little Dreamer in March of 2021.

Her dream to be a humanitarian worker, as well as interests in education, mental health and equality inspire many of her poems and quotes. Through Ella's passion for people, reform, and harmony, she wishes to help others own their identity, take a stand, forgive, unite, and ultimately heal.

In 2018 Ella launched The Leadlight Project, as a creative hub for teens struggling with social isolation and loneliness. The Projects aim, to gather identified teens to develop and create artwork, poetry, short films, and photography to be showcased and celebrated at a collaborative exhibition, scheduled for the 12th of October 2019, in conjunction with QLD Mental Health. Unfortunately, due to ongoing illness, Ella had to place the Project's collaborative Exhibitions on hold. In 2021, the re-formatted project relaunched via a new Shopfront whereby a percentage of sales will be donated to children's charities dear to Ella's heart, including Unicef's Yemen Crisis.

www.ellazelensky.com

Divine Decree ISBN 978-0-6450978-2-5
Divine Decree e-book ISBN 978-0-6450978-3-2
© Ella Zelensky, 2021. All rights reserved

notes

www.ingramcontent.com/pod-product-compliance
Lightning Source LLC
Chambersburg PA
CBHW012335300426
44109CB00047B/2546